*...and forbid not
to speak with
tongues*

...and forbid not to speak with tongues

By

Howard M. Ervin

LOGOS INTERNATIONAL
185 NORTH AVE.
PLAINFIELD, N.J. 07060

By Special Arrangement With
PARACLETE PUBLICATIONS
Hazlet, N.J.

Revised Edition

#759809

Dedicated to

to

My Parents

"their children shall

rise up and call

them blessed"

FOREWORD TO THE SECOND EDITION

This little volume began as a personal correspondence with a former parishioner. The story is briefly told in the Foreword to the first edition. The problems it dealt with recurred with increasing frequency in the context of a growing charismatic ministry, and a limited private circulation in mimeograph form seemed the logical next step in answer to this felt need.

It soon became apparent that the needs to which it was addressed were more than local, or even regional. The consequence was a printed first edition which passed through three printings.

After the third printing, it seemed to those who controlled its destiny that its mission was accomplished. For several years it has been "out of print," but not out of demand. Finally, in the face of continuing requests for it, the decision was made to reissue it. However, experience indicated that certain literary revisions were desirable to increase the readability of the text. In addition, a maturing charismatic experience pressed for a clarification of some of the areas touched upon.

Even so, the changes have been surprisingly

few. Style and content remain essentially the same.

With the heart-felt prayer that its message will continue to assist others in their "walk in the Spirit," these letters which are known familiarly to many as the "Letters to Tony" are sent forth in fresh garb.

3 January, 1969

Howard M. Ervin
Tulsa, Oklahoma

FORWORD TO FIRST EDITION

The following letters were originally addressed to a young friend from our Emmanuel Fellowship, who, at the time of writing, was a student in a Bible Institute. Deeply troubled by the violent prejudices against the experience of the baptism in the Holy Spirit, which he encountered among numerous Evangelical Christians, he wrote to me, as his pastor, for counsel. Included in one of his letters was a booklet by the Rev. Dr. J. Vernon McGee, Th.D., entitled *Talking in Tongues*. My young colleague had, by underlining, and by questions jotted down in the margins, focused attention upon those arguments in the booklet which particularly disturbed him.

The first of these letters was directed to answering his questions . . . and the doctrinal views that had evoked them. The second letter is a sequel to the first. In it attention is called to additional arguments on the same theme advanced by Dr. M. R. De Haan, M.D., in his booklet, *Speaking in Tongues*. A portion of a third letter is included, because it supplements the interpretation of several of the Biblical passages touched on in the first two letters.

Because of an increasing awareness that others are also perplexed, even misled, by these unscriptural and ofttimes extravagant arguments against the baptism in the Holy Spirit — particularly against the Biblical phenomenon of "tongues" — these letters are herewith shared with a larger audience. The few editorial changes, introduced into these printed copies, have not changed the informal style of argumentation employed, nor materially affected the content. The author can but pray that they will be of some assistance to those who, though hungry of heart, have been hindered in their search for the fulness of Divine Blessing by human opinions and biases. To such, we would say, do not allow a prejudice to rob you of a blessing. At least, read the following pages with an open heart and mind, and may the Holy Spirit of truth lead you into a fuller knowledge of Jesus Christ who said, "I am . . . the truth."

20 December, 1962

Howard M. Ervin, Th.D.
Pastor
Emmanuel Baptist Church
Atlantic Highlands, N.J.

an open letter to a questioning believer

additional insights from Pastor Ervin

a final word

...an open letter to a questioning believer...

(rebuttal to questions raised by Dr. J. Vernon McGee's booklet, *Talking in Tongues*)

EMMANUEL BAPTIST CHURCH

Memorial Parkway & 7th Avenue
Atlantic Highlands, N.J. 07716

Dear Tony:

Greetings in the precious Name of Jesus (Phil. 2:9-11). Thank you for your good letters, and for sharing your burdens and problems with us. Our Emmanuel Fellowship rejoices in your stand on the baptism in the Holy Spirit. We are praying much for you. God is faithful. God is able. Praise His holy Name! (I Cor. 10:13; Heb. 2:18). We are looking forward to your return to Emmanuel. It will be a blessing to share with you, out of God's Word, and out of our own experience, all that we know He has for you.

Thank you also for sending along Dr. J. Vernon McGee's booklet, *Talking in Tongues*. My reactions to it will be set forth at some length in the succeeding pages. May I preface my analysis of the author's arguments by calling attention to the biased and polemic viewpoint that pervades the whole treatment of the subject. It cannot, therefore, be impartial and objective in the conclusions presented. As a consequence, my rebuttal of these conclusions will inevitably assume the tone of an "apology" (defense).

The author's particular theological bias is patently Dispensationalism. I am calling your attention to this because his conclusions are the logical consequences of his theological presuppositions. They are not the product of objective Biblical research.

In an effort to help you to see the truth more clearly, I shall try to answer the questions you raise in your underlining of the text and in your marginal notes.

The *ad hominem** argument with which the author introduces his subject, I will pass over since it is unworthy of a Christian, and all the more objectionable when used to discredit the witness of fellow believers. I have come to know a number of ministers and laymen in this interdenominational Full Gospel movement, and have found them to be men deeply taught in the Scriptures, and completely "sold out" to our Lord and Saviour Jesus Christ.

---

*Webster's Collegiate Dictionary, ed. 1942: "ad hominem. To the man; - of an argument directed at one's prejudices rather than one's intellect." In practice, it is often resorted to in order to evade the force of an opponent's argument by attacking his character, motives, ability, etc. Thus it seeks to destroy the credibility of his witness without answering his argument.

We shall begin with your underlining of the following statement on page 4 of the booklet.

"The Corinthian church was made up of baby believers. Paul called them 'babes in Christ' and he called them carnal. It was among them that this had broken out. They were guilty of many things, and one thing was that they were abusing the gift of tongues."

This is true in part, but consider the context, I Cor. 3:1-3. "And I, brethren, could not speak unto you as unto spiritual, but as unto carnal, as unto babes in Christ. I fed you with milk, not with meat; for ye were not yet able to bear it: nay, not even now are ye able; for ye are yet carnal: for whereas there is among you jealousy and strife are ye not carnal, and do ye not walk after the manner of men?" Please note carefully, that Paul does not call them "carnal" and "babes" because they were "speaking in tongues," but for the heresy of schism and party spirit, (I Cor. 1:10-13). What the author (and the other opponents of the baptism in the Holy Spirit who repeat this specious argument) fails to see is that the Bible expressly says, that "speaking in tongues" is a self-manifestation of the Holy Spirit, (I Cor. 12:7, 1:10ff); but "schism" and "party-strife" are manifestations of the flesh (I Cor. 1:10-13). Note further that these schisms were fostered by teachers, not by tongues. Now if Paul referred to the Corinthian believers as "carnal" and "babes in Christ" for their schisms and party spirit, how much worse would modern Christianity with its multiplicity of "splits" and "factions" appear to him!

It is right at this point that the absolute necessity for the revival of the "gifts" of the Holy Spirit, including "tongues," comes into clearer focus. Notice that in I Cor. 12:1-11, the apostle Paul discusses nine gifts of the Holy Spirit. In I Cor. 12:12-27, he interprets the unity of the Church under the similitude of the organic unity of the body. Then I Cor. 12:28-31 briefly sets forth the application of the "gifts" as "ministries" within the Body of Christ. This order is not by mere happenstance, I can assure you. There is a vital spiritual purpose in it, for the "gifts" minister supernaturally to the maintaining of the unity of Christ's Body, His Church.

Tony, I can say this in all humility and gratitude to Jesus, that it was the "baptism in the Holy Spirit," with the subsequent manifestations of the "gifts" of the Holy Spirit (including the blessed manifestation of "tongues"), that has redeemed and purified my own understanding of, and deepening appreciation for, the unity of all believers in Christ.

The next point to be considered is brought out by your underlining of the following quotation on page 6.

"Now what is the explanation for all this? Are we returning to apostolic days or are we going into days of apostasy? Is Pentecost being

6

*repeated today? Have the sign gifts returned to
the church? If so, where are the thousands of
converts such as those who were the fruit of the
original sign gifts when the church began at the
day of Pentecost?"*

The question as put above is merely rhetorical. Again, the author fails to weigh objectively the facts of Scripture, and contemporary experience. For example, we read of the apostolic Church, that: "These all with one accord continued steadfastly in prayer, with the women, and Mary the mother of Jesus, and with his brethren" (Acts 1:14). The clue is in the words, "all with one accord." Let the Church be united as it was at Pentecost, and it will conquer spiritually and irresistibly the citadel of "Man-soul." Satan's strategy has always been divide and conquer, and it is long since past time, that we believers awaken to this fact, and stop our civil war within the Body of Christ. As I said above, it is precisely this that the Holy Spirit is now accomplishing through the baptism in the Holy Spirit. Never have I, personally, been so conscious of the unity of believers as I have been since being filled with the Holy Spirit in a "Pentecostal" experience, and "speaking in tongues." As "tongues" at the Tower of Babel divided mankind, even so, the "tongues" given supernaturally by the Holy Spirit serve to unite Christians now.

Just ponder for a moment the cruel and unjust attacks launched by some leaders against Evangelist Billy Graham, and against their own Christian brethren who are in the Full Gospel movement. What reaction must this "civil war" within the Body of Christ have upon unbelievers when they hear of it? Is it any wonder that the Holy Spirit is grieved at the lack of love and unity among Christians? Certainly, the first task of the Holy Spirit, in this modern "Pentecostal outpouring" of the Holy Spirit, is to purify and to unite Christian believers before global mass evangelism will be a reality. In spite of this lamentable disunity among Christians, recent statistics on the Pentecostal movement in South America, published in *Time* magazine, show that the Pentecostals are by far the largest, and fastest growing, Evangelical groups in Latin America. I feel that a recent experience here at Emmanuel will be helpful to you in this regard. Several weeks ago two young sailors were brought to our church by Ed and Ann Dorsett. They attended services for about three weeks while their ship was docked at the Earle pier. Both received the baptism in the Holy Spirit before leaving us. About a week later, Ed and Ann received a letter from Tex and Jerry saying that they had already led seven or eight of their shipmates to the Lord, and were starting a Bible class aboard ship. Both attribute these victories to the new power in witnessing they received through the baptism in the Holy Spirit. I wonder why opponents of the baptism in the Holy Spirit stress the three thousand souls saved after Peter's sermon at Pentecost, but ignore the meager results of Paul's preaching on Mars Hill. Yet Paul, too, was "filled" with the Holy Spirit, spoke with tongues more than any of the believers at Corinth (I Cor. 12:18), and wrought signs and wonders. This selective use of the Scripture evidence, by the author, reflects a large element of "special pleading" that must, by its very nature, miss the truth.

The next question to be considered is contained in your marginal notation on page 8. It was apparently prompted by the following statement of the author.

"There is a profound and appalling ignorance of the Bible in the modern tongues movement that cannot make you rejoice."

Relative to this, you ask in the margin: "How much ignorance? I must know. I'll go halfway with him here. Emmanuel knows the Bible, but what about the rest of the 'tongues speaking' people? Has Emmanuel been taken in by ignorant men, deceived, or are there other tongues speaking churches who know the Bible?"

Here I can speak out of a very recent experience. In mid-September, I was one of forty denominational ministers at a clergy retreat near Columbus, Ohio. All these ministers were invited because they had been filled with the Holy Spirit in a "Pentecostal" experience. During the three or four days of the retreat we lived constantly in the atmosphere of the apostolic Church. The "gifts" of the Holy Spirit were in evidence. As for the Bible teaching, never have I heard deeper or more pro-

9

found expositions of the Bible. Were these men scholars in the Word? Yes! Some even used their Nestle's Greek Testaments fluently in the meetings to follow the teaching being given. There were Episcopalian, Baptist, Methodist, Presbyterian, Lutheran, Reformed, Mennonite, and one Pentecostal minister in attendance. Never have I heard even my Fundamentalist brethren "plead the blood of Jesus" as these brethren did in prayer. And such love for God's Word as they displayed would make your heart rejoice. Thank God for such men who are growing in grace and in the knowledge of Jesus, and are leading their churches in the same paths.

Your next question on page 9 is closely related to the foregoing one. It was prompted by this statement of the author.

"Many sincere people are hungry and they do not know where to go for food in this hour. In their desperation they turn to any direction and they eat anything that is put before them, as a starving man would."

You have noted in the margin this question: "This may not be true about Emmanuel, but what about the others, I ask again."

Dear Tony, I categorically and emphatically deny that Dr. McGee's generalized indictment is true of Emmanuel. I would further add that it is not true of the denominational ministers whom I know in the Full Gospel movement. They do not "turn to any direction," and "eat anything that is

put before them as a starving man would do."
They are turning to the Word of God, and feeding
upon the "Bread of Life." It is in the pages of
God's precious Word that they find the truth of
the baptism in the Holy Spirit, and humbly appro-
priate "the promise of the Father" for themselves.
I have only answered this *ad hominem* argument of
the author because it seemed to trouble you.
Actually the generalizations the author makes here
come perilously close to slander of good and godly
brethren. I am afraid that this may sound unchari-
table on my part. If so, it is not intended to be so,
but is a consequence of the type of answer necessi-
tated by the author's charges.

The next point you have underlined is this one,
also on page 9. Referring to the testimony of Rev.
Marvin Buck, the author commented:

> "*You will notice that he (Rev. Buck)
> omitted from his quotation of that verse (Mk.
> 16:17), 'They shall take up serpents, and if
> they drink any deadly thing, it shall not hurt
> them.' I insist that they drink the poison and
> they pick up the snakes, because it all goes
> together.*"

The author's exegesis here borders on the sin
of presumption. To be consistent, he must also in-
sist that Peter, Paul, and the rest of the apostles did
the same thing. Does he class the apostles with
snake handlers? This is true of some Indian fakirs, I
am told. I emphatically repudiate the implication

11

that the apostolic Church belongs in this category. Surely Paul's experience with the snake on the island of Melita, Acts 28:1-6, is an inspired, and sufficient, exegetical safeguard for the objective and reverent exegesis of Mark 16:18. I realize that the way in which I have said this may sound harsh. I do not intend it to be so, but am at a loss to adequately characterize the sheer casuistry of the author's "exegesis" in this place.

A third underlining is also found on page 9.

"As I searched the literature of the tongues movement, I found that instead of being based on the Word of God, it is based on experience. Always there is an experience, and an experience that is put over against the Word of God."

This I emphatically deny. The experience stems from the Word of God. It never supplants, nor contradicts, the Scriptures. For myself, I came to the truth of the infilling with the Holy Spirit, as distinct from the operation of the Holy Spirit in conversion and regeneration, as far back as 1951, solely through a study of God's Word. I saw its truth through a careful, and painstaking, verse by verse exegesis of the book of Acts. Furthermore, I stand ready to assist any earnest, unbiased, inquirer to understand this precious truth, as presented in God's Word. We accept only one authority for the validity of the experience, and that authority is the Holy Bible.

12

The next place you have underlined is on page 10.

> *"The manifestation of tongues has figured in present day cults, and is still being practiced in heathen religions. My friend, you cannot trust your feelings, you cannot trust your experiences. God has given us His Word, and by it every experience and doctrine should be tested — not by just a few 'proof texts,' but by a careful study of the context. If this experience is dominating your spiritual life, you should know what place in the total Word of God has been given to this matter of tongues."*

Apparently the writer forgets that "discerning of spirits" is also a "gift" of the Holy Spirit. Can a reverent understanding of what Scripture says about "tongues" really confuse them with the psychic manifestations of spiritualism and other psychic cults? Acts 2:4 contains a simple test: "And they were all filled with the Holy Spirit, and began to speak with other tongues as the Spirit gave them utterance." Note that the act of speaking was under their control. They did the speaking. The Holy Spirit supplied the words.

Biblical "speaking in tongues" is clearly distinguishable from demonically inspired psychic phenomena by the application of this simple Biblical principle. The Holy Spirit never abridges the autonomy of the human will. The "spirit of the prophets is subject to the prophets" (I Cor. 14:32).

13

The "speaker in tongues" is in control of the speaking, for "if there be no interpreter [present] let him keep silence . . . speaking [i.e., in tongues] to himself, and to God." (I Cor. 14:28). On the other hand, in the demonically inspired psychic manifestations of non-Christian cults the speaker surrenders his will to the complete domination of an alien personality. Frequently, this is manifested in a catatonic or trance state, as in spiritualism.

The writer's plea, that this matter be judged in the light of the context, I heartily endorse, but it works both ways. For example, in an effort to prove that the Scriptures consider "tongues" as the least of the gifts, he quoted (page 19) I Cor. 14:19, as support for his thesis. This matter will be treated again later on, but note here how he has violated his own dictum on the use of "proof texts." In his quotation of I Cor. 14:19 apart from I Cor. 14:18, he has dismembered the sentence to serve a polemic purpose. This is the more blameworthy since he quoted the ASV in this place. This Version places the first word of verse 19 in the lower case, e.g., "howbeit." Since, however, the author quotes it in capitals, i.e., "Howbeit," he gives the impression that it is the beginning of a new sentence. Actually, verse 19 is a continuation of the sentence begun in verse 18. Observe carefully what is then omitted by this arbitrary treatment of the passage. I Cor. 14:18: "I thank God I speak with tongues more than you all: (14:19) howbeit in the church I had rather speak

14

five words with my understanding, that I might instruct others also, than ten thousand words in a tongue."

As for the author's plea, that the place of tongues be considered in the light of the total Word of God, I most heartily concur. This is, however, a large order, that neither Dr. McGee's book let, nor my reply can hope to do, in such limited space. Therefore, Tony, when you have finished my letter, it will be up to you to decide which one of us has dealt the more faithfully with the Scriptures.

On page 11 of the booklet you have raised a question concerning the following:

> "Likewise on the day of Pentecost the Holy Spirit came. The sound as of a rushing mighty wind, and the tongues like as of fire were manifestations that never were repeated, for the Holy Spirit never came again — He was here. He had begun His work, which He is continuing today, of forming the body of believers that we know as the Church. Some have said that there was a second Pentecost — a Gentile Pentecost — in the home of Cornelius when Peter presented the gospel there. But of course it was not a Pentecost in any sense of the word — there was no sound of wind or appearance of fire, the Holy Spirit did not come again, for He was here."

The point that is really at issue here is the writer's statement, that what happened in the house of the Gentile centurion, Cornelius, "was not a Pentecost in any sense of the word." His attempt to justify this by the argument that the sound of wind, and appearance of fire were absent, is another example of sheer casuistry. The central reality of Pentecost is the indisputable fact of a "Pentecostal experience." Believers were filled with the Holy Spirit in a definite experience. Judge the author's claim in the light of Peter's express statement to the church at Jerusalem when he described what had happened in Cornelius' house: "And as I began to speak, the Holy Spirit fell on them, even as on us at the beginning" (Acts 11:15). Dr. McGee argues, in essence, that what happened in the home of Cornelius was in no sense a "Pentecostal experience." Peter said they received the same experience as the disciples on the day of Pentecost. You must decide which to accept as true.

We pass now to page 12 where you have called attention to the following:

> "The thing that took place was super-natural, and I personally believe it was supernatural speech, not supernatural hearing. Rather than being an 'unknown' tongue, they were speaking in languages understood by these people from different areas of the Roman Empire."

Here the confusion results, not so much from what is said, but from what is left unsaid. The "tongues" spoken by the disciples at Pentecost were known to those who heard and understood them as their native languages. But the languages being spoken by the disciples were unknown to the disciples. The bystanders recognized and commented on the fact, saying, "are not all these Galileans, and how hear we, every man in his own language." (Acts 2:7, 8).

Read this in the light of Paul's statement, I Cor. 14:14: "For if I pray in a tongue my spirit prayeth, but my understanding is unfruitful." That is to say, when Paul spoke in tongues, they were "unknown" languages to him, but not to any listener who happened to know the particular language in use. Even Paul did not know the languages he spoke "in the Spirit," but this did not stop him from speaking in tongues, for he adds, (vs. 15): "What is it then? I will pray with the spirit [i.e., in tongues], and I will pray with the understanding also. I will sing with the spirit [i.e., in tongues], and I will sing with the understanding also." Furthermore, Paul refers to the tongues [languages] of men, and of angels, in I Cor. 13:1. There must, therefore, be celestial languages, distinct from earthly languages, which may or may not be intelligible to men. This experience happened to me when I was praying for a missionary who understood Spanish. Recently one of our women, at a cottage prayer meeting, prayed in tongues. An Italian engineer who was present heard and understood her as she prayed in both Italian and Latin, yet the woman in question does not know either language.

Your next underlining is found on page 12.

"In the book of I Corinthians, the practice of tongues is dealt with because it was being used in excess and it was being abused in the Corinthian church."

Here I am somewhat at a loss to see what bearing this has on the author's thesis, that the sign gifts ceased with the apostolic age. Does the author mean to imply from this (as other opponents of the baptism in the Holy Spirit do) an argument for the discontinuance of speaking in tongues? I get this impression as I read the context. If so, it would be just as logical to ban the Lord's Supper, because they abused that too at Corinth. Some of the believers there came to the Lord's Table drunk (I Cor. 11:21).

Paul felt constrained to regulate the public manifestation of tongues lest the "unbelievers" and the "unlearned" ("him that is without gifts," footnote ASV) be caused to stumble (I Cor. 14:23). But Paul also says, "and forbid not to speak in tongues" (I Cor. 14:39)—hardly then an argument against the proper use of tongues.

Please observe carefully what else Paul said about tongues, and the desirability thereof. "Now I would have you all speak with tongues, but rather that ye should prophesy, and greater is he that prophesieth than he that speaketh with tongues, except he interpret, that the church may receive

18

edifying." In passing, observe carefully why. Paul here rated "prophecy" above "tongues." In I Cor. 14:4 he says that the one speaking in a tongue edifies himself, while the one who prophesies builds up the whole church. Therefore, since one of the prime purposes in the worship service is to edify the whole company of believers, the "gift" that accomplishes this is given preference. Paul is not making a value judgment upon the intrinsic value of any of the "gifts" of the Holy Spirit. His judgment, as to relative importance, is dictated by the practical needs of the public assembly. But even here tongues is not subordinate, if there be an interpretation coupled with it, "that the church may receive edifying" (I Cor. 14:5).

The paragraph immediately preceding the quotation above has an even more significant error which you overlooked; but because of its importance I am calling your attention to it here.

> "There is a third and last reference to speaking in tongues, which occurs in chapter 19 of Acts. Paul had gone to Ephesus where he found a group of people who thought they were Christians because they had heard through Apollos the message of John the Baptist. Paul detected that they were not indwelt by the Holy Spirit of God, and began to make inquiry. When he found that they were not saved, he gave them the gospel and they received Christ. You can well understand that these people were certainly confused, because they had previously thought they were Christians. Now an evidence

19

> *of their salvation is necessary. 'And when Paul had laid his hands upon them, the Holy Ghost came on them; and they spake with tongues, and prophesied (Acts 19:6)'."*

The conclusion arrived at here is another example of the confusion in which the theological presuppositions of the author enmesh one. If one equates the "Pentecostal" baptism in the Holy Spirit with salvation, then one must of necessity, I suppose, rationalize "tongues" and "prophecy" as evidences of salvation. But this is perilous theologizing, to say the very least.

Let us see just what the Word actually reveals in this place. Read carefully Acts 19:1-7. Watch the sequence of events. Paul first instructed the Ephesian disciples about Jesus. Acts 19:5 says: "And when they heard this, they were baptized into the name of the Lord Jesus." Scripturally, water baptism follows conversion. We can be reasonably certain then that Paul did not baptize these twelve men in water until he was sure they were saved (regenerated). Then after their water baptism, we read: "And when Paul had laid his hands upon them, the Holy Spirit came upon them: and they spake with tongues, and prophesied."

What is the significance of the laying on of hands here? Compare the experience of the Samaritans (Acts 8), whom Philip led to the Lord, and then baptized in water (Acts 8:12). Some time later, Peter and John were sent down by the church at Jerusalem and, when they came to Samaria, they laid their hands upon these Samaritan converts, and "they received the Holy Spirit" (Acts 8:17). Were these Samaritan believers also "confused" and in need of a supernatural "evidence of their salvation"? Remember Paul's own experience when Ananias laid his hands upon him in Damascus (Acts 9:17), and Paul received his sight, and was filled with the Holy Spirit (Acts 9:17-19). In the face of such plain Biblical teaching one cannot seriously believe that the laying on of Paul's hands on the twelve Ephesian believers, and their resultant speaking in tongues and prophesying, was evidence of salvation. It was, rather, evidence of the supernatural "filling" or "baptism" in the Holy Spirit. Scores of times we have seen the same thing repeated. Hungry believers have come to us seeking a deeper experience with God, the Holy Spirit. After prayer, and the laying on of hands, we have heard them speak "with other tongues, as the Spirit gave them utterance" (Acts 2:4).

The burden of proof for the statements made in the next place you have underlined, pp. 13-14, rests with Dispensational theologians.

"Very little, therefore, is in the Scriptures relative to tongues. What we do have in the New Testament occurs during the great transitional period. The great transition is between law and grace. It began with the ministry of our Lord Jesus who was born under the law, "made under the law" (Gal. 4:4). He is the One who

21

> *prepared His disciples, and it took Him three years to prepare them, for this great transition from law to grace. It continued through the ministry of not only Paul the apostle, but of John the apostle. There were sign gifts during this transitional period. You will notice in the literature of the modern tongues movement a great deal is said about sign gifts. But, may I say, the sign gifts were for the period of transition."*

This period of transition exists only in the theology of Dispensationalism. It is as unscriptural as other theories of this system, e.g., their view that there is a "Jewish Dispensation" in the book of Acts. The evidence marshalled here in this paper should be sufficient to demonstrate the utterly unscriptural nature of the claim that the "sign gifts were for the period of transition"; as well as showing the wholly supposititious nature of this nonexistent "period of transition." Compare again Acts 2:39 where the "Pentecostal" promise is "to all that are afar off, even as many as the Lord our God shall call unto him." If God is still "calling," the "promise" is still in effect.

A second question is also raised by our underlining on page 14.

> *"Paul and the other apostles had the sign gifts also. They had the sign gifts because they did not have what you and I have today—the Word of God. When Paul started out with the gospel message, nothing of the New Testament*

*had been written. Paul himself wrote the
second book of the New Testament. When he
went into a new territory with his message,
what was his authority? He had no authority
except sign gifts. Notice Paul's own statement:
'Truly the signs of an apostle were wrought
among you in all patience, in signs, and
wonders, and mighty deeds' (II Cor. 12:12).
May I say to you, my friend, if you can find an
apostle living today then you will find signs.
But there are no apostles living today – the sign
gifts died out with the apostles."*

Note two fallacies here. Paul did have the
Word of God. In every synagogue Paul entered he
preached Jesus as Messiah, and Saviour, from the
only Scriptures the Jews would have recognized as
authoritative, viz., the Old Testament. Remember
the commendation of the Jews in Berea, (Acts
17:11): "Now these were more noble than those in
Thessalonica, in that they received the word with
all readiness of mind, examining the scriptures
daily, whether these things were so." This is
exactly what Jesus did on the road to Emmaus as
He conversed with the two disciples on the resurrection day. "And he said unto them, These are my
words which I spake unto you, while I was yet
with you, that all things must needs be fulfilled,
which are written in the law of Moses, and the
prophets, and the psalms, concerning me. Then
opened he their mind, that they might understand
the scriptures . . . " (Luke 24:44,45).

The second fallacy, in the quotation above, is

23

the view that the "sign gifts" were the exclusive prerogative of the apostles, used only to accredit the apostolic authority. What then of Ananias, an otherwise unknown believer, who laid hands on Paul, and healing, and the filling with the Holy Spirit resulted. Or again Philip, who was a deacon, not an apostle; yet in Samaria "multitudes gave heed with one accord unto the things that were spoken by Philip, when they heard, and saw the signs which he did. For from many of those that had unclean spirits, they came out crying with a loud voice: and many that were palsied, and that were lame, were healed" (Acts 8:5,6). Furthermore, Jesus said that "these signs shall accompany them that believe" (Mk. 16:17). In other words, "sign gifts" were the common possession of all believers, as Jesus said they would be, for their daily witness. They were never only a prerogative of the apostles. They were to be a confirmation of the preaching of His word, by all believers.

Please observe carefully the remark quoted above from Dr. McGee's booklet (page 14), viz., "the sign gifts died out with the apostles." On page fifteen, three lines after this categorical statement, he concedes the following: "I am willing to grant that on many mission fields today some of these gifts appear."

I protest! The author cannot have it both ways at one and the same time. If, as he categorically claims, "the sign gifts died out with the apostles," then these gifts cannot appear on the mission fields today, nor anywhere else for that matter. If, as he concedes, they do appear on the mission fields today, then they have not ceased with the age of the apostles — or do we still have apostles after all! The contradiction here is amazing, yet only what one would expect. This contradiction reveals the irreconcilable tensions implicit in Dispensationalism when confronted with the facts of Christian experience, and the explicit statements of the Word of God.

Immediately after the above statement, the author continued by saying (page 15):

"I think that tremendous miracles have been wrought on pioneer mission fields, but not in Los Angeles where the written Word and the spoken Word are available on every hand. The signs were given to make the Gentiles obedient."

One is tempted to ask then whether there are no more Gentiles to make obedient to the Gospel? This doctrinaire exaltation of the written Word, divorced from the plenitude of the Holy Spirit's activity in His ninefold gifts (I Cor. 12:4ff) and fruit (Gal. 5:22f), makes one vulnerable indeed to the accusation of the Liberals that we Conservatives worship a "paper pope."

To adequately deal with the question you raise on page 18, I shall have to quote extensively from the booklet.

25

"We have seen the importance of sign gifts at the beginning of the transitional period. But these gifts disappeared. You may say to me, 'Are you sure they disappeared?' I want to say to you categorically and emphatically, that the sign gifts disappeared and the Scriptures said they would. Let me give you Phillips translation of I Corinthians 13:8,9: 'For if there are prophecies they will be fulfilled and done with, if there are 'tongues' the need for them will disappear.' Now while I do not recommend Phillips translation as a translation, it is an excellent interpretation and in this case gives us Paul's exact meaning — the need for tongues will disappear. Tongues will cease. He continues, 'if there is knowledge it will be swallowed up in truth.' That is, there will be no longer the necessity for giving Scripture. The time will come when Scripture will end. When John wrote Revelation he said in effect, 'Don't add any more and do not take anything from it. We are through. It is finished.' And by the same token tongues have ended."

Here again, the author's conclusions are no better than his assumptions. He has not shown, either from the verses quoted or from the context, when "prophecy," "tongues," and "knowledge" are to cease. The argument used to support his contention is that "knowledge" (I Cor. 13:8) is synonymous with the giving of Scripture; therefore, the completion of the canon of the New Testament marks the end of this gift in the Church. On what Biblical authority does the author define the "gift of knowledge" thus?

My rebuttal is very simple. Nowhere in the context of the passage referred to does Paul even vaguely intimate that the "gift of knowledge" was to be equated with the giving of Scripture, or the completion of the New Testament canon. This is a dogmatic assumption that has no Biblical justification.

On the other hand, we may legitimately ask whether Paul does, in the context, indicate when these three gifts are to cease. I believe he does quite clearly in I Cor. 13:10,12, i.e., "but when that which is perfect is come, that which is in part shall be done away . . . For now we see in a mirror, darkly; but then face to face: now I know in part; but then shall I know fully even as also I was fully known." Paul here confessed the fragmentary nature of his knowledge, and eagerly anticipated the time when he, personally, along with the rest of the Church, should "know fully." To equate this with the completion of the canon of the New Testament is not exegesis but eisegesis (i.e., the reading into the text a meaning the author did not intend). The time obviously in view here is the Parousia (Second Coming) of Jesus Christ, and not the end of the apostolic age. Just for a moment, recall Paul's words in I Cor. 14:22: "Wherefore tongues are for a sign, not to them that believe, but to the unbelieving." We still have the "unbelieving" with us. We still witness to an unbelieving race of men. Granted this truth, then the need for tongues as a "sign" to unbelievers has not diminished by one iota since the days of the apostles. We need the "sign" of supernatural "tongues" just as much now as they did then.

No one who is acquainted with the facts of Church History can possibly hold the view that the sign gifts ceased with the apostolic age. Nor can any amount of prejudice change the record. A helpful summary of the witness of Justin Martyr, Irenaeus, Tertullian, Origen, etc., is found in A. J. Gordon's book, *The Ministry of Healing*, pp. 58ff. Get it and read it. Dr. Gordon begins chapter IV, p. 58, with the following quotation from Dr. Gerhard Uhlhorn. "Witnesses who are above suspicion leave no room for doubt that the miraculous powers of the apostolic age continued to operate at least into the third century." Lester L. Riber, D.D., in an article in *Trinity Magazine*, Trinitytide, 1962, p. 31, records the following: "In Saver's [*sic*. Sauer's] *History of the German Church*, Vol. 3, page 406, the following words are found: 'Dr. Martin Luther was a prophet, evangelist, speaker in tongues, and interpreter, in one person, endowed with all the gifts of the Spirit.' "

The following quotation to which you call attention on page 18 of Dr. McGee's booklet is very important.

"The conclusion we come to is that speaking in tongues is not an evidence of the baptism of the Holy Spirit. The baptism of the Holy Spirit was never functional, it was organic and vital. 'By one Spirit are we all baptized into

28

one body, whether we be Jews or Gentiles,
whether we be bond or free (I Cor. 12:13).' "

Two points are raised here. First, observe that
Peter, and the Hebrew Christians with him, in the
house of Cornelius knew "that on the Gentiles also
was poured out the gift of the Holy Spirit. For
(*gar*, a conjunction used to express cause, etc.)
they heard them speak with tongues and magnify
God." Could it be put more plainly than this, that
speaking in tongues is evidence of the baptism in
the Holy Spirit? Acts 2:4 certainly bears this out:
"And they were all filled with the Holy Spirit, and
began to speak with other tongues, as the Spirit
gave them utterance." Therefore, to say that speaking in tongues is not evidence of the baptism in the
Holy Spirit is an unequivocal denial of a truth
clearly affirmed in Scripture. Consult the gospels
and you will find that the apostles wrought
miracles at our Lord Jesus' commission before Pentecost. But, the distinguishing miracle of the
"Pentecostal experience," in which all the disciples
in the upper room were filled with the Holy Spirit,
is speaking in tongues. Does it not strike you as
significant, even important, that of the nine "gifts"
of the Holy Spirit listed in I Cor. 12, the first to
appear at Pentecost was speaking in tongues? Jesus
said, "ye shall be baptized in the Holy Spirit not
many days hence" (Acts 1:5). When this promise
was fulfilled in the outpouring of the Holy Spirit
on the day of Pentecost, the writer of the book of
Acts says: "And they were all filled with the Holy

Spirit, and began to speak with other tongues, as the Spirit gave them utterance" (Acts 2:4). I submit that the Biblical evidence admits of no other conclusion than that speaking in tongues is evidence of the baptism in the Holy Spirit.

In the second place, notice his conclusion based on I Cor. 12:13: "The baptism of the Holy Spirit was never functional, it was organic and vital . . . We all have been put by the Holy Spirit into the body of believers — that is the baptism of the Holy Spirit. It takes place the moment you trust Chrisr as your Saviour" (p. 18). To properly evaluate this argument we must consider the whole of I Cor. 12:13: "For in one Spirit were we all baptized into one body, whether Jews or Greeks, whether bond or free, and were all made to drink of one Spirit." Note the two verbs, "we were baptized," and "we were made to drink." Both, in the original, are aorist passive forms, which means that the action takes place upon the subject.

Two relationships to the Holy Spirit are set forth here. These may be interpreted in three possible ways. One: some see here the twin sacrament of Baptism and the Lord's Supper. Two: Dispensationalism must either ignore the second verb (which is the usual procedure in their literature that I have seen), or else say that both are synonyms, referring to the same event, namely, conversion. Three: the first verb refers to conversion, when one is immersed in the Spirit, and placed in the Body of Christ. Now notice the second verb, "were made to drink." This represents a second relationship to the Holy Spirit. In this relationship the believer is the "vessel," as it were, into which the Holy Spirit is imbibed.

J. W. Shepherd in *The Life and Letters of St. Paul*, p. 248 footnote, quotes Dr. Robertson (a famous Baptist scholar) as saying of this second verb: "First aorist pass. ind. of *potizo*, 'made to drink.' Here Paul refers to the imbibing of spiritual gifts." I Cor. 12:13 then sets forth two relationships of the believer to the Holy Spirit, (1) baptism = regeneration, and (2) drinking in = imbibing of the charismatic fulness of the Holy Spirit.

It will be well here to pursue the meaning of "baptize" a step further. We might ask if this use of the word in I Cor. 12:13 establishes the meaning of the word in Acts 1:5. For Dr. McGee, along with other anti-Pentecostal writers on the subject that I have read, it apparently does. He assumes that because the word "baptize" in I Cor. 12:13 refers to conversion, therefore it must have the same meaning in Acts 1:5. Applying the author's rule, that the baptism of the Holy Spirit takes place the moment one trusts Christ as Saviour, one is forced to the inevitable conclusion that the disciples were not born again until Pentecost.

Let me say it again for emphasis: if the baptism in the Holy Spirit and conversion (regeneration) take place at the same time, then the disciples were not born again until Pentecost. Is this true? Did not the disciples believe on Jesus before Pentecost? Note Romans 10:9, 10: "because if thou shalt confess with thy mouth Jesus as

Lord, and shalt believe in thy heart that God raised him from the dead, thou shalt be saved: for with the heart man believeth unto righteousness; and with the mouth confession is made unto salvation." Observe that belief in the resurrection is here a precondition of salvation. Inasmuch as the disciples were baptized in the Holy Spirit at Pentecost, was this when they believed in Christ, and in His resurrection? Remember that according to Dr. McGee, the baptism in the Holy Spirit takes place the moment you trust Christ as your personal Saviour. Could the disciples have had fellowship with Christ during forty days of post-resurrection appearances, and have stood with Him upon the Mount of Ascension, watching Him being taken up into heaven, and still not have believed in His resurrection until Pentecost? The suggestion strains the limits of one's credulity. Surely the fallacy of the writer's argument should be obvious by now.

To clarify it even further, does the Bible suggest a time when the disciples did believe in Christ, and in His resurrection? Yes, I believe it does. Notice John 20:19-23: "When therefore it was evening, on that day, the first day of the week, and when the doors were shut where the disciples were, for fear of the Jews, Jesus came and stood in the midst, and saith unto them, Peace be unto you. And when he had said this, he showed unto them his hands and his side. The disciples therefore were glad, when they saw the Lord." (Eight days later this was repeated for the benefit of Thomas who was absent from the upper room on the resurrection day. When he saw the wounds in Jesus' body he said: "My Lord and my God," vs. 28. Hence, visible proof of the resurrection produced faith.) "Jesus therefore said to them again, Peace be unto you: as the Father hath sent me, even so send I you. And when he had said this, he breathed on them, and saith unto them, Receive ye the Holy Spirit: whose soever sins ye forgive, they are forgiven unto them, whose soever sins ye retain, they are retained." If the baptism in the Holy Spirit takes place the moment one trusts in Jesus, then why did the disciples have to wait fifty days until Pentecost to be baptized in the Holy Spirit? They had obviously believed in Jesus and His resurrection when they saw that He had been raised from the dead. The conclusion is equally obvious. The attempt to prove that conversion and the baptism in the Holy Spirit in Acts 1:5 are conterminous is futile and erroneous.

Now consider carefully what transpired after Jesus proved His resurrection to His disciples according to John 20:19ff: "he breathed on them, and saith unto them, Receive ye the Holy Spirit." This cannot be, as some have said, an anticipation of Pentecost. The tense of the verb "receive" (aorist) does not refer to a future event, but indicates immediate reception.

The account of the creation in Gen. 2:7 suggests why Jesus "breathed" upon them in the upper room on the resurrection day. "And Jehovah God formed man of the dust of the ground, and breathed into his nostrils the breath of life." By the act of "breathing," God conferred life upon Adam, and on the resurrection day Jesus "breathed" upon the assembled disciples and conferred spiritual life (regeneration) upon them. Remember further, that in the Genesis record God gave man dominion over the created sphere (Gen. 1:28), after "breathing" life into him. So, too, after Jesus "breathed" spiritual life into His disciples in the upper room on the resurrection day, He gave to them dominion in the spiritual realm (John 20:23). Certainly the parallel is highly suggestive.

One last word here. In Acts 1:8, Jesus specifically defined the baptism in the Holy Spirit as a baptism for power, not regeneration. If we receive at conversion "the baptism in the Holy Spirit," where is the power Jesus said would result from this baptism (Acts 1:8)? How desperately we all need the power of the Holy Spirit in these last days! How long will Christians cherish a theological prejudice and lose a blessing? Would that all Christians would humbly acknowledge the Church's powerlessness of life and witness (Fundamentalists as well as Liberals) and seek the baptism in the Holy Spirit. This is the way ordained by our Triune God—Father, Son, and Holy Spirit—for the Christian to receive power to glorify Jesus.

Another question raised by the author on page 18 is based upon his personal experience, rather than upon Scripture.

> *"There are no second class Christians, all have been placed into the body of Christ. The claim of a special baptism of the Holy Spirit ministers to pride. Oh, the letters I have received that reflect this! But, my friend, there are no second rate Christians."*

Pentecostals have no monopoly on "pride." Reading the above quotation reminds me of the words of our Lord Jesus: "He that is without sin among you, let him cast a stone at her" (John 8:7). This is again an example of the *ad hominem* argument to which we have had to call attention before. It is an attack upon individuals, rather than upon their faith and doctrine. Its purpose is to impeach the character and motives of one's opponents; and thus, by inference, to cast a slur upon the truth to which they bear witness. The conclusion it seeks to instill is this. "Many Pentecostals are guilty of the sin of pride; therefore, the 'Pentecostal experience' is false because it ministers to pride." Such an accusation, "from the seat of the scornful," leveled against those who have received the baptism in the Holy Spirit, is itself the very essence of pride. To suggest that someone else's pride is worse than one's own pride is but to acknowledge one's own guilt. But pause here a moment. Suppose this charge were true of some who had received the "Pentecostal experience." Does their failure prove the experience is Scripturally wrong? How many "born again" Christians have brought disrepute upon the Gospel by scandalous lives! Does their misconduct prove the Gospel is wrong? Even worse, does their sin mean that the Gospel is responsible for their sinful lives? Odious as such a suggestion is, it is precisely the accusation Dr. McGee levels against the Biblical experience of the baptism in the Holy Spirit.

Tony, it saddens one to see the lengths to which Christians will go in attacking other Christians with whom they happen to differ doctrinally. In truth, the greatest burden we have had to bear since receiving the baptism in the Holy Spirit is the attacks of other believers. Truly, such conduct in the household of faith must make the wounds of Jesus to bleed again.

The last objection I shall deal with relates to the relative value of speaking in tongues, page 19. The author writes:

> *Secondly, from these three chapters (I Corinthians 12, 13, 14) we learn that tongues was an inferior gift. Even in the days of the apostles it was considered so. 'And God hath set some in the church, first apostles, secondarily prophets, thirdly teachers, after that miracles, then gifts of healing, helps, governments, diversities of tongues (I Cor. 12:28).' Tongues is listed last. Paul makes it more emphatic by adding in chapter 14: 'Howbeit in the church I had rather speak five words with my understanding, that I might instruct others also, than ten thousand words in a tongue (I Cor. 14:19 ASV)."*

Please observe very carefully the consequences of failure to pay attention to the whole context of the passage in question (I Cor. 12, 13, 14). The above quotation is based upon a pseudo-exegetical rule of last mention, viz., "tongues are mentioned last; therefore, they must be the least of the gifts." Let us apply this principle to I Cor. 13:13. Notice that Paul places "love" last. "But now abideth faith, hope, love, these three . . ." If we apply the fallacious rule of last mention here, as Dr. McGee does to tongues in I Cor. 12:28, then we would be driven to the conclusion that love is the least of the fruit of the Spirit because it is mentioned last. But remember that Paul adds "and the greatest of these is love."

Now to expose completely the fallacy of this "rule of last mention," let us reverse the application of it. The result would be something like this. Paul mentions "love" last in I Cor. 13:13 because, as he says, it is the most important. Therefore, since tongues are mentioned last in I Cor. 12:28, tongues must be the most important of the gifts of the Holy Spirit. The author's contention that tongues is the least of the gifts because it is mentioned last is therefore not true. Recall what we have said before about the importance of tongues as revealed in other passages we have examined and you will be much closer to the truth.

Just a few more comments relative to the author's use (or misuse) of I Cor. 14:19 in the foregoing quotation. Refer again to our remarks on page 12 of this letter to refresh your memory of our discussion of this very passage. Remember that we called attention there to the fact that the author had ignored the first half of the sentence beginning with I Cor. 14:18: "I thank God, I speak with tongues more than you all . . ." Does such a statement sound as though Paul were here underrating the importance of tongues? Of course not! Recall again that Paul said that tongues is the "gift" with which we edify ourselves (I Cor. 14:4). With this in mind, look again at I Cor. 14:19: "howbeit in the church I had rather speak five words with my understanding, that I might instruct others also, than ten thousand words in a tongue." My good friend, Rev. David DePlessis, has aptly remarked, that if Paul did not speak in tongues in church, where then did he speak his ten thousand words in a tongue? Obviously at home in private worship. Then having edified himself with prayer in tongues, before he went to church, he only needed five words in the language current among the believers to get the work done.

No, Tony, Paul does not here imply a value judgment on the relative inferiority of tongues, or any other gift of the Holy Spirit. He recognizes rather that each manifestation of the Holy Spirit has its proper place in the total ministry of the Holy Spirit to the Church. Refer again to page 16 of this letter where this fact is discussed. May the Holy Spirit guide you and open the eyes of your understanding as you study the truths set forth in this "epistle."

The rest of the questions you raise on pages

19-20 of the booklet under discussion here pertain to the author's subjective summation of his particular theological bias, and need not detain us longer. There are no considerations of any exegetical consequence here to require a rebuttal. I believe that I have answered as completely and concisely as possible the pertinent objections to the baptism in the Holy Spirit presented in the booklet. When you get home I shall look forward to sitting down with you and showing to you the wealth of Biblical evidence supporting the baptism in the Holy Spirit. It is much too voluminous to do by letter.

Sincerely yours in Christ,
s/ Pastor Ervin

— NOTES —

— NOTES —

... *additional insights from Pastor Ervin*

(rebuttal to statements made by Dr. DeHahn in *Speaking in Tongues*)

EMMANUEL BAPTIST CHURCH

Memorial Parkway & 7th Avenue
Atlantic Highlands, N.J. 07716

Dear Tony:

This is a sequel to my last letter. It occurs to me that I ought to write to you again to supplement what was said there about the baptism in the Holy Spirit. Dr. McGee did not include all the objections one meets with in the anti-charismatic literature; therefore, I shall include some additional views set forth by Dr. DeHaan in his booklet, *Speaking in Tongues*.

It is also an opportunity to share with you additional insights from I Corinthians 12, 13, 14. We begin here with I Cor. 12:1-3.

"Now concerning spiritual gifts, brethren, I would not have you ignorant. Ye know that when ye were Gentiles ye were led away unto those dumb idols, howsoever ye might be led. Wherefore I make known unto you, that no man speaking in the Spirit of God saith, Jesus is

anathema; and no man can say, Jesus is Lord, but in the Holy Spirit."

Beginning with the first phrase, "Now concerning spiritual gifts," the first thing we notice is that the word "gifts" does not occur in the original Greek text. It has been supplied by the translators. In the Greek text, the word "spiritual" may be either masculine or neuter in gender. If taken as masculine, the subject to be discussed is "spiritual persons." One commentator renders it thus: " 'concerning the men of the Spirit' (speakers with tongues)." (This interpretation is found, among others, in Meyer's *Critical and Exegetical Handbook to the Corinthians*, 1884, p. 275.) On the other hand, if the word "spiritual" is taken as a neuter, it then refers to "spiritual gifts (or manifestations)," in line with I Cor. 12:4ff. Either interpretation is grammatically possible, but both lead to the same ultimate conclusion. Whether the reference is to "those who exercise spiritual gifts," or to the "gifts" (charismata) themselves, this central fact emerges: the context deals with the place of these "gifts" as supernatural endowments for life and service, particularly in the worship and service of the Church. This supplies the basis for an understanding of all that follows in I Corinthians 12, 13, 14.

In the light of the subject announced in verse one, the contrast in verses two and three between "dumb idols," and "speaking in the Spirit of God," bears a significant relationship to the subject of "spiritual gifts." It is the phrase "speaking in the Spirit" that commands attention here. We must arrive at some understanding of its meaning before proceeding further. Let us pause to ask ourselves what the phrase, "speaking in the Spirit," really means. To answer our question we must consider its relationship to its context. How is this phrase, "speaking in the Spirit," related to the subject of "spiritual, i.e., supernatural, gifts"? Does the context throw any light upon our question? To ask the question is to suggest the answer. The answer probably rests with one of the specific "speech gifts" listed among the "gifts" of the Holy Spirit in I Cor. 12:4-11, e.g., either "prophecy," or "tongues," or "interpretation of tongues."

Broadening our examination of the context helps us to narrow the possibilities before us even further. I Cor. 14:2 suggests an answer consistent with what we have already observed. "For he that speaketh in a tongue speaketh not unto men, but unto God; for no man understandeth; but in the spirit he speaketh mysteries." I am sure that you will see immediately that Paul here identifies "speaking in a tongue" with "speaking in the spirit." However, the question must now be faced whether or not "speaking in the spirit" here is the same phenomenon as in I Cor. 12:3. Let us examine this question more closely. Two interpretations of the phrase "in the spirit," I Cor. 14:2, are possible. First, the reference here is to the Holy Spirit, in which case the phrase is identical with that in I Cor. 12:3. The fact that the translators wrote "spirit" in lowercase letters instead of capitalizing it thus, "Spirit" = the Holy Spirit, merely reflects their interpretation. Second, the "spirit" referred to is the speaker's own spirit, not the Holy Spirit (cf. I Cor. 14:14). In this event, we then understand with Alford, (*Greek Testament*, vol II, 5th ed., p. 590) "his spirit is the organ of the Holy Spirit." But here again either choice leads to the same conclusion, namely, that the speaking originates with the Holy Spirit, and the utterance is heard as "tongues." From this Biblical evidence we conclude that "speaking in the Spirit" (I Cor. 12:3) means "speaking in tongues," as the context in I Cor. 14:2 demonstrates.

I submit then, that what Paul is really saying in I Cor. 12:3 could be paraphrased something like this: "No man speaking in tongues, supernaturally given by the Holy Spirit, will say that Jesus is accursed, even as no one can profess Jesus as Lord in a language he understands except his profession be likewise energized by the same Holy Spirit." Let me say here, as I have already pointed out in my former letter, that the "gift" of "supernatural tongues" known in Scripture is that given by the Holy Spirit.

Since most commentators are agreed that in this epistle Paul is answering a number of questions submitted to him by the Corinthian Christians, we naturally wonder what question prompted Paul to write: "no man speaking in the Spirit of God saith, Jesus is anathema; and no man can say Jesus is Lord, but in the Holy Spirit." The suggestion is made by some commentators that these represented rallying cries of Jews and Christians in the synagogue. That is to say, the Jews cried, "Jesus is anathema (accursed)." To this the Christians replied, "Jesus is Lord." I, personally, reject this solution because there is hardly a demonstrable relationship with the subject announced in verse one, and developed in the ensuing context, viz., "spiritual, i.e., supernatural gifts." Instead, it introduces a subject which is foreign to the context. However, when we see that "speaking in the Spirit" has reference to speaking in "tongues," another solution presents itself. Were the believers at Corinth troubled by the accusations of their opponents who intimated that since they did not understand the languages they were speaking "in the Spirit" they were in danger of cursing Jesus when they spoke in "tongues"? If so, then Paul wrote this rebuttal to reassure them saying, that it is impossible for a Christian "speaking in the Spirit," i.e., in "tongues," to curse Jesus. Nor is this solution at all far-fetched. (It becomes even more plausible when judged by the frequency and bitterness with which this accusation is lodged against the contemporary manifestation of "tongues" among Christians. It is a continuing source of bewilderment to me to understand the "logic" by which that which was orthodox at Pentecost becomes heterodox in Christian assemblies today. I refer, of course, to the attitudes and accusations of those who oppose "tongues" for today.)

Consider the following citation from Dr. DeHaan's booklet, page 3, where he levels this same charge against the Corinthian church.

"Instead of using this God given gift [the author is referring to "tongues"] for its spiritual purpose, they made it the occasion for carnal spiritual pride and self-exaltation and often made it the test of really being saved and having the Holy Spirit.

"From verse three we infer the awful extremes to which it had led. Here is the verse.

" 'Wherefore I give you to understand, that no man speaking by the Spirit of God calleth Jesus accursed; and that no man can say that Jesus is Lord, but by the Holy Ghost.'

"Some blasphemous and wicked utterances by individuals, under the spurious ecstacy of so-called "tongues" were uttered as having been inspired by the Spirit of God Himself. The name of Jesus was the most common expression among them. It was Jesus, Jesus, Jesus, while they rejected His Lordship and His authority. They evidently seldom or never used the name, Lord Jesus, but only the name Jesus."

This whole quotation is simply an incredible series of gratuitous assumptions without relation to the text quoted, or demonstrable foundation in fact. Please observe that by the author's own admission these conclusions, offered in the name of Bible teaching, rest solely upon inferences drawn from his theological presuppositions, rather than upon verifiable Scriptural exegesis. We are justified — yea more, obligated — to ask, therefore, upon what Biblical grounds the author accuses them of "carnal spiritual pride and self-exaltation" in their use of "tongues." Paul wrote to the Corinthian church, "concerning spiritual gifts, brethren, I would not have you ignorant." Now "ignorance," i.e., lack of knowledge, or misunderstanding, concerning these "gifts" is not the same as "carnality."

Dr. DeHaan repeatedly belabors the point of the "carnality" and "spiritual immaturity" of the Corinthian church. He says, for example, page 8:

> "In conclusion, therefore, let me remind you that the gift of tongues was most prominent in the most carnal of churches. God gave the gift to the weakest, most immature, childish believers at Corinth until they should grow up and become mature and have no more need for special manifestations."

A strange inconsistency becomes apparent in Dispensational teaching at this point. The assertion is repeatedly made in Dispensational literature that this is the Laodicean age of the Church. Read again in Revelation 3:14ff of the fearful carnality of the Laodicean church, and of God's judgment upon it: "I will spew thee out of my mouth." Carnal as it

51

may have been, God never said this about the church at Corinth. If Dispensationalists really believe, as many of them declare, that the present age is the Laodicean age of the Church, then the contemporary Church (Fundamentalists and Liberal and all shades between) is even more carnal than the Corinthian church at its worst. If then carnality and immaturity are the prerequisites for the manifestation of "tongues," (if it is carnal, immature, childish believers who need tongues to help them mature) then such a revival of "tongues" is long overdue in the present "Laodicean church." Without embracing the presuppositions of Dispensationalism that suggest this conclusion, I do heartily believe that the Divine cure for our present spiritual apathy and impotence in the Christian Church is the baptism in the Holy Spirit accompanied by all the "gifts" of the Spirit.

However, just to keep the record straight, may it be said again that Paul did not charge the Corinthians with being carnal because they spoke in "tongues," but because of schism and party-spirit (I Cor. 1:10ff), jealousy and strife (I Cor. 3:1ff). These schisms were caused not by "tongues" but by "teachers."

Having come to grips with I Corinthians 12:1-3, we are ready now to proceed. Take your Bible and read again I Cor. 12:4-11. Here Paul lists nine "gifts" of the Holy Spirit, e.g., "the word of wisdom," "the word of knowledge," "faith," "gifts of healings" (please note that it does not say "gifts to be healers," as it is so often misconstrued to

52

mean), "workings of miracles," "prophecy," "discernings of spirits," "kinds (varieties) of tongues = languages," "interpretation of tongues." Now observe carefully the purpose for which the Holy Spirit dispenses these gifts. "But to each one is given the manifestation of the Spirit to profit withal." To profit whom, one asks? To profit the whole assembly of believers is the answer of Scripture. Tony, keep this verse in mind. It is a summary of God's basic purpose in giving the "gifts" of the Holy Spirit, viz., "to profit withal"; and believe me, after almost twenty years of pastoral experience, I know something of the desperate need of the Church to profit from these "divine endowments," now more than ever.

Of these nine "gifts" of the Holy Spirit, "tongues" is the one most commonly misunderstood, and misrepresented. It is also the "gift" most bitterly assailed by many Christians.

In an attempt to discredit "tongues," those who oppose the baptism in the Holy Spirit try to show that the "tongues" spoken at Pentecost and the "tongues" spoken at Corinth were not the same spiritual phenomenon. Dr. DeHaan says quite categorically, pages ten and eleven:

"Now this manifestation of the day of Pentecost was not the same as the gift of tongues in I Corinthians 12 and 14. These apostles did not speak in UNKNOWN tongues, but in the known languages of the people to whom they spoke (p. 10).

53

> *"From this, therefore, it will be perfectly apparent that the apostolic speaking in tongues at Pentecost and the 'Sign' of tongues at Corinth have nothing in common at all, but were totally different experiences" (p. 11).*

Tony, in my former letter I replied to Dr. McGee's misuse of this same specious argument. Read it again to refresh your memory. One last word may be added here to what was said there. Six times in I Corinthians 14, the King James Version translates "unknown tongues." In not one single instance, however, is the word "unknown" substantiated by the Greek text. In some copies of the King James Version, this fact is recognized by placing the word "unknown" in italics. Dr. DeHaan, on pages 11, 12, 13, and 14 of his booklet, quotes four of these examples. However, he omits any acknowledgement of the facts just cited, viz., that the word "unknown" has been inserted by the translators, and simply reflects their interpretation. In view of the importance that Dr. DeHaan attaches to the "UNKNOWN tongue" at Corinth, his failure to note this fact represents a curious default in scholarship. As it stands, his mere quotation of these verses lends tacit approval to his thesis.

The only textual justification for the view that the "tongues" spoken at Corinth were "unknown" is I Cor. 14:2: "For he that speaketh in a tongue speaketh not unto men, but unto God; for no man understandeth; but in the spirit he speaketh mysteries." The phrase, "no man understandeth," may be interpreted in one of two ways. First, in a general sense as categorically affirming that there is no one anywhere who could understand, and translate what was being said in "tongues." Second, in a specific sense, that no one present in the Corinthian assembly could understand what was being said thus. Here again the context assists us in deciding the most probable interpretation.

I Corinthians 13 is an integral part of the total context dealing with "spiritual gifts." This chapter opens with a verse that has something of vital importance to say on the subject of the "UNKNOWN tongue." Here Paul wrote, I Cor. 13:1a: "Though I speak with the tongues (languages) of men and of angels . . . " What does Paul mean when he refers here to the "languages of men and of angels"? Obviously to an experience known to himself, and to the Corinthians to whom he wrote. These were the "tongues" being spoken at Corinth, as well as by Paul himself. Paul clearly indicates in this place that the "gift of tongues" includes both earthly and celestial languages. The celestial languages may, or may not, be intelligible to men. This is not the point at issue here. But the "tongues of men" are earthly languages, spoken and understood by men. Whenever the Holy Spirit enables one to speak "the tongues of men," these are languages intelligible to, and translatable by, those who know and speak the languages in question. I say with complete confidence that the "gift of tongues" is one and the same manifestation of the Holy Spirit whether manifested in Jerusalem, at Pentecost, or in Corinth, or in Atlantic Highlands, New Jersey. I can say this on the basis of Scripture, the interpretation of which has been enriched for me by this very experience as it unfolds in my own life.

From his erroneous assumption that the "tongues" spoken at Pentecost were a totally different manifestation from the "tongues" spoken at Corinth, Dr. DeHaan deduces the following fallacious conclusion, pages 10 and 11.

"The 'Pentecostal' manifestation of tongues was never again repeated. If the Pentecostal gift of tongues were for us today, none of our missionaries would have to spend any time in language study. They could then go to a foreign land and immediately begin preaching to these people in their own languages without any previous preparation. The apostles did just this on the day of Pentecost."*

*Compare this statement with Acts 11:15. Peter reported back to the Church at Jerusalem: "And as I began to speak the Holy Spirit fell on them, even as on us at the beginning" (i.e., at Pentecost). How did Peter know this? Because "they heard them speak with tongues and magnify God" (Acts 10:46). Since Peter declared that the Holy Spirit fell on the household of Cornelius in the same manner as He had upon the Church at Pentecost, then by parity of reason we may affirm that the same experience produced the same manifestation in tongues.

56

Since Dr. DeHaan unqualifiedly declares that the disciples preached the gospel in "tongues" at Pentecost, we are justified in asking then whether or not the Bible supports this view. The answer is a categorical no! Consider this express statement of those who heard them speak in "tongues," Acts 2:7, 8, 11: "And they were all amazed and marvelled, Behold, are not all these that speak Galileans? And how hear we, every man in our own language wherein we were born? . . . we hear them speaking in our tongues the mighty works of God." Notice that it is "the mighty works of God," not the gospel. They were not preaching the gospel in "tongues": they were praising God for all His mighty works. Compare here the supportive evidence of Acts 10:46. When the Holy Spirit fell upon Cornelius and his household, Peter, and the Hebrew Christians with him, "heard them speak with tongues, and magnify God." Notice carefully, "and magnify God." Once again, the speaking in "tongues" is praise. Peter preached the gospel: Cornelius and his household spoke in "tongues." If the speaking in "tongues" is for the preaching of the gospel, to whom did Cornelius, and his household, here preach?

Now note two things. One, both at Pentecost, and again in the home of Cornelius, the speaking in "tongues" was heard as praise. Second, if these were the kind of "unknown tongues" Dr. DeHaan insists occurred after Pentecost, how did Peter and those with him know what Cornelius and his household were saying in "tongues"? Return to

Acts 2 for a moment. It was after the manifestation of "tongues" at Pentecost that Peter preached the gospel to the multitudes, Acts 2:14-40. What language did Peter probably use to proclaim the gospel? A logical assumption is Aramaic, the language that would be understood by nearly all those present at Jerusalem at that time. Remember too, that in Mark 16:17ff, "tongues" are not for the preaching of the gospel, but constitute one of the supernatural "signs" that accompany and confirm the preaching of the gospel. This is precisely the position the "tongues" occupy in relation to the preaching of the gospel in the account of Pentecost contained in Acts 2.

Rather than trying fruitlessly to discredit "tongues," may I suggest a much more edifying approach to the subject, albeit also a much more positive one. Tony, have you ever studied the Scriptural reasons for "tongues? If not, I am sure it will be a pleasant surprise to see the blessed ministry this supernatural manifestation of the Holy Spirit performs. I shall suggest seven Biblical reasons for speaking in "tongues."

1. "Tongues" are a sign that confirms the witness of believers to the Word of God. Mark 16:17, 18, 20: "And these signs shall accompany them that believe: in my name shall they cast out demons: they shall speak with new tongues; they shall take up serpents, and if they drink any deadly thing, it shall in no wise hurt them; they shall lay hands on the sick, and they shall recover . . . And they went forth, and preached everywhere, the Lord working with them,

and confirming the word by the signs that followed. Amen."

2. "Tongues" are a vehicle of praise to God. Acts 2:7, 11b: "And they were all amazed and marvelled, saying . . . we hear them speaking in our tongues the mighty works of God." Acts 10:45, 46: "And they of the circumcision that believed were amazed, as many as came with Peter, because that on the Gentiles also was poured out the gift of the Holy Spirit. For they heard them speak with tongues, and magnify God."

3. "Tongues" are a supernatural means of speaking to God in prayer. I Cor. 14:2: "For he that speaketh in a tongue speaketh not unto men, but unto God; for no man understandeth; but in the spirit he speaketh mysteries."

4. "Tongues" are a means of self-edification (not inflation, in spite of charges to the contrary). I Cor. 14:4: "He that speaketh in a tongue edifieth himself; but he that prophesieth edifieth the church." (Review what I said about this verse in my former letter. Self-edification is needful and desirable, when it is done in the privacy of one's own prayer closet.)

5. "Tongues" are a sign to unbelievers. I Cor. 14:22: "Wherefore tongues are for a sign, not to them that believe, but to the unbelieving; but prophesying is for a sign, not to the unbelieving, but to them that believe." This is the other side of the truth in Mark 16:17ff. There the stress is laid upon our Lord's presence with believers in this sign. Here the emphasis is on the effect produced upon believers. On

one occasion I prayed with a Japanese Buddhist woman for the healing of her little daughter. However, since the greatest miracle God performs is the "new birth" — it is literally a resurrection from the dead — I first spent three-quarters of an hour explaining the plan of salvation to her. Despite her limited knowledge of English, she later told the friends who had brought her to me that she understood everything I said. This was in itself a miracle. After prayer for her daughter, they drove her home. On the way she suddenly said to them, "I want your Jesus." It was not until a week later that they found out what prompted her statement. She told them that when we prayed for her daughter she heard me pray in Japanese, and God spoke to her through me in her native language — a convincing "sign gift."

6. "Tongues" are a supernatural means of taming the "restless evil" of the tongue. James 3:8: "But the tongue can no man tame; it is a restless evil, it is full of deadly poison." (Read the whole paragraph here relating to the tongue, James 3:1-12.) Tony, this is so terribly true of all of us. But this I know, that while speaking in "tongues" it is the Holy Spirit that controls my tongue, and He will say nothing displeasing to God or man.

7. Tongues are often a means of ministry to believers. For example, some months ago a missionary on furlough came to me to be anointed with oil and prayed for for healing. This missionary speaks Spanish, having served in Mexico and in the Philippines. I never studied Spanish, consequently, I do not know the language. However, as I prayed for this missionary "in the Spirit," she heard me pray in a

Spanish dialect, "Father be propitious to this needy soul" (her translation). Later there was more in the same language about sin. I have three Christian eyewitnesses for this fact, in addition to the missionary.

Having referred to I Cor. 13:1 above, a further word is in order here. So often this thirteenth chapter is wrenched from its context and made to say something, I am sure, the apostle Paul never intended. For example, "love" is not the greatest of the "gifts" (charismata) of the Holy Spirit. "Love" is a "fruit" of the Holy Spirit. Compare I Cor. 12:4-11 with Gal. 5:22,23. The "fruit" of the Spirit is an expression of the very nature and character of God, while the "gifts" reveal the personality of God in supernatural operation.

Ponder carefully this statement. Remember that the Bible says, "God is love," I John 4:16. This is the very essence, the very nature of God. Note, furthermore, that each of the "gifts" of the Holy Spirit are expressions of personality in action. For example, knowledge, faith, speech are predicates of personality. It is necessary to see this to understand what Paul is saying about the charismata of the Holy Spirit. I Cor. 12:31 concludes with these words: "And moreover a more excellent way show I unto you." Tony, what is the "most excellent way" of which Paul speaks? Is it "love" without, or perhaps superseding, the "gifts"? Read I Cor. 13:1 again: "If I speak with the tongues of men and of angels, but have not love, I am become sounding brass, or a clanging cymbal." Observe here very, very carefully that it is the divorcing of the "fruit" of the Spirit from the "gifts" of the Spirit that produces such severe condemnation from the Apostle. But now, read Paul's statement as an affirmative. Suppose I speak with the tongues of men and of angels, and I have love too. What then is the result? That is to say, suppose I manifest both the "fruit" and the "gifts" of the Holy Spirit. What are we to conclude then? I submit that the answer is "this is the most excellent way" spoken of by Paul in I Cor. 12:31.

Peter summarized his "Pentecostal sermon" with these words, Acts 2:38, 39: "And Peter said unto them, Repent ye and be baptized every one of you in the name of Jesus Christ; and ye shall receive the gift of the Holy Spirit. For to you is the promise, and to your children, and to all that are afar off, even as many as the Lord our God shall call unto him."

First, let us consider the words, "and ye shall receive the gift of the Holy Spirit." Should there be any question about the nature and the manifestations accompanying this "gift of the Holy Spirit," the events that transpired in the house of Cornelius should settle such questions, once and for all. Cf. Acts 10:45: "because that on the Gentiles also was poured out the gift of the Holy Spirit." In the house of Cornelius, as well as at Pentecost, the reception of the "gift of the Holy Spirit" was attested by the supernatural sign of "speaking with other tongues." You see, when one receives "the gift of the Holy Spirit," as the disciples did at Pentecost, and as Cornelius and his household did, they receive the Holy Spirit in a dimension of radically dynamic spiritual power. In regeneration all believers receive the Holy Spirit, and His presence is attested by the manifestation of His "fruit." (In my last letter, I pointed out to you that the disciples received the Holy Spirit in regeneration on the resurrection day, John 20:22. In the upper room, before Pentecost, we see evidence of the "fruit" of the Holy Spirit in their lives. They "with one accord" — the unity of the Spirit, Eph. 4:3 — "continued steadfastly in prayer.") In the baptism of the Holy Spirit, believers enter a new, and supernatural dimension of power in the Holy Spirit, as attested by His "gifts."

Return now to Acts 2:39 quoted above. "For to you is the promise, and to your children, and to all that are afar off, even as many as the Lord our God shall call unto him." Peter undoubtedly refers here to the Pentecostal experience, which was the occasion for his "Pentecostal sermon." This is indicated by the close contextual relation between "the promise," Acts 2:39a, and "the gift of the Holy Spirit," Acts 2:38b; " . . . and ye shall receive the gift of the Holy Spirit. For (because) to you is the promise . . . " That is to say, "the promise" = "the gift of the Holy Spirit." Thus the context makes it clear that Peter here refers to the experience of Pentecost. Notice the almost identical statement of our Lord Jesus when He announced the coming of the Pentecostal "baptism in the Holy Spirit." Acts 1:4, 5: " . . . he charged them not to depart from Jerusalem, but to wait for the promise of the Father . . . for John indeed baptized with water; but ye shall be baptized in the Holy Spirit not many days hence." A significant part of that Pentecostal experience was "speaking with other tongues, as the Spirit gave them utterance."

Consider then the scope Peter here envisaged for this experience. "For to you is the promise" (that is, to the assembled multitude), "and to your children" (that is, to their descendants), "and to all that are afar off, even as many as the Lord our God shall call unto him." Tony, God is still calling men unto Himself. The "promise" is still in effect, and upon this fact Dispensationalism founders in its attempt to "Dispensationalize" Pentecost out of the Church today. God purposes that His Church experience and manifest both the "fruit" and the "gifts" of the Holy Spirit. The Divine Purpose, as revealed in the Bible, is for the manifestation of both the "fruit" and the "gifts" of the Holy Spirit in the life, and in the witness of the Church today, and until Jesus comes again.

Throughout this letter I have examined, and answered, some of the opinions set forth by Dr. DeHaan in his booklet, *Speaking in Tongues*. Since he repeats much the same arguments as Dr. McGee, I have not attempted a systematic rebuttal of his viewpoint. Rather, I have confined my remarks to those places where he adds something not found in Dr. McGee's booklet on the subject.

There is one more such example from Dr. DeHaan's statement of his position that I want to analyze for you. The following citation is found on pages 16 and 17:

> *"Paul definitely infers here that these signs were (for ?) those who were still babes in their understanding of the full truth of the grace of God. Tongues in Corinth were for folks with weak faith. Paul says so in verse 22:*

> *" 'Wherefore tongues are for a sign NOT to them that believe, but to them that believe NOT.'*   *I Cor. 12:22*

> *"We must stop right here because these words are important and hold the key to the entire situation. First of all Paul is talking only about born again believers. It is important to remember this. No unconverted person can have the genuine gift of tongues or any other gift of the Spirit for it is a spiritual gift and the unbeliever is spiritually dead. So let us remember that he is talking about born again believers only. But he divides these Christian born again believers into two groups. 'Those saints who believe' and 'Those saints who believe not.' Two different words are used in the Greek. The word used in the first phrase,*

> *" '. . . tongues are for a sign, not to them that believe . . . '*   *I Cor. 12:22*

> *" '. . . but to them that believe not . . . '*   *I Cor. 14:22*

> '   *"The word is 'apistos' and means one who*

*does not fully trust. It may be translated
'doubter', so that the passage would naturally
read,*

*" 'Wherefore tongues are for a sign, not to them
who fully trust the Lord, but to them who still
doubt.'* I Cor. 14:22"

The author's conclusion, viz., that "he (Paul) is talking about born again believers only . . .'Those saints who believe,' and 'Those saints who believe not,' " rests solely upon the translation he claims for "apistos," i.e., "doubter." If this translation is false, so also is his conclusion. Yes, and more than this, his whole argument is false for he says that his interpretation of this verse "hold(s) the key to the entire situation." The question to be asked, and to be answered here, is this: What is the meaning of "apistos"? Please forgive me if I seem tedious at this point. To prove beyond any shadow of doubt that "apistos" cannot here mean "a born again believer . . . a saint who doubts," I shall include a list of Greek language authorities, with their translations, to support my contention.

1. Arndt & Gingrich, *A Greek-English Lexicon of the New Testament,* p. 85; "faithless, unbelieving. Especially of the heathen . . . I Cor. 14:22."

2. Liddell & Scott, *A Greek-English Lexicon,* p. 173; "in N.T., unbelieving, an unbeliever."

3. Thayer, *Greek-English Lexicon of the New Testament*, p. 57; "without faith or trust, unbelieving, incredulous: of those who refuse belief in the gospel, I Cor. 14:22."

4. *The Classic Greek Dictionary*, p. 83; "of persons, faithless."

5. Young, *Analytical Concordance to the Bible*, p. 1012; "disbelieving, disobedient." He lists nine times that "apistos" is used in the New Testament. In not one instance can it bear, even remotely, the sense given to it by Dr. DeHaan.* Even more to the point is Paul's use of the word "apistos." Young's *Concordance* lists five occurrences of the word in I and II Corinthians. In not one single instance can the word be legitimately forced to bear the meaning assigned to it by Dr. DeHaan.

Quite obviously then, Dr. DeHaan is in error when he says that "apistos" means a "doubter," i.e., "born again believers . . . saints who believe not." Furthermore, since this is, in his own words, "the key to the entire situation," he has made his position to stand or to fall on the meaning he has

---

*The use of "apistos" by our Lord Jesus in John 20:27 offers no support for the interpretation adopted by Dr. DeHaan. It cannot be proven that Thomas was a "Christian born-again believer" at the time Jesus addressed him thus in the upper room. In the light of Rom. 10:9 and 10 the opposite was true.

claimed for the word "apistos." The consequences are disastrous for his whole thesis. Since his premises are wrong, his conclusions must inevitably be wrong. The overall result is the discrediting of his entire teaching on the Holy Spirit as set forth in this booklet.

May the full blessing of our Triune God—Father, Son, and Holy Spirit—be your portion. At this Advent season, we are praying that your Christmas will be a blessed one, and may the New Year be filled with fruitfulness in your life for the glory of our blessed Lord Jesus Christ. Maranatha!

Sincerely yours in Christ,
s/ Pastor Ervin

– NOTES –

– NOTES –

...a final word

or

the Word is Final

... *finally*

EMMANUEL BAPTIST CHURCH

Memorial Parkway & 7th Avenue
Atlantic Highlands, N.J. 07716

Dear Tony:

It is encouraging to us to know that you find the most recent issue of *Trinity Magazine* interesting. We sent it to you in the hope that it would prove helpful to you, and to your interested friends.

I am most grateful to you for enclosing the anonymous criticism of my former letters to you ... As a matter of fact, Tony, my position on this question is broadly based in the Scriptures. I submit the three following examples which should make this fact amply clear:

1. Let me call attention to Acts 8. This is the record of the great revival in Samaria in which Philip was the human instrument that God used. Acts 8:12 says: "But when they believed Philip preaching good tidings concerning the kingdom of

God and the name of Jesus Christ, they were baptized both men and women." Is it not obvious that these Samaritan converts were saved (i.e., regenerated)? They believed on Jesus, and were baptized in water by Philip. This certainly satisfied the requirements for "believer's baptism." Next observe, that in Acts 8:14-17 we read: "Now when the apostles that were at Jerusalem heard that Samaria had received the word of God, they sent unto them Peter and John; who, when they were come down prayed for them, that they might receive the Holy Spirit: for as yet He was fallen upon none of them: only they had been baptized into the name of the Lord Jesus. Then laid they their hands on them and they received the Holy Spirit."

Follow closely the sequence of events. Conversion and "believer's baptism," then sometime later (i.e., the time necessary for news of the revival to travel from Samaria to Jerusalem, and for the Church there to send Peter and John down to Samaria) Peter and John came down and, Acts 8:17, " . . . laid they their hands on them, and they received the Holy Spirit." The sequel is, in one sense, cryptic, yet nonetheless suggestive. Acts 8:18, 19: "Now when Simon saw that through the laying on of the apostles' hands the Holy Spirit was given, he offered them money, saying, Give me also this power, that on whomsoever I lay my hands, he may receive the Holy Spirit."

Question. What did Simon "see" that convinced him that the Christians there had received the Holy Spirit? Such a stalwart of orthodoxy as

Adam Clarke in his *Commentary*, says of Acts 8:18: "By hearing these speak with different tongues and work miracles (Vol. I, p. 741, ed. 1837). Meyer, in his *Handbook to the Acts of the Apostles*, says: "The communication of the Spirit was visible . . . in the gestures and gesticulations of those who had received it, perhaps also in similar phenomena to those which took place at Pentecost in Jerusalem" (p. 171). Meyer quotes Calvin in the same vein: "Calvin on verse 16 writes 'Surely Luke speaketh not in this of the common grace of the Spirit, whereby God doth regenerate us, that we may be His children; but of those singular gifts, wherewith God would have certain endued at the beginning of the gospel to beautify Christ's kingdom' " (p. 180). (I would wholeheartedly endorse Calvin's view, here expressed, with the single exception that Acts 2:39 does not limit it to "the beginning of the gospel," but says rather that this experience is for " . . . as many as the Lord our God shall call unto him.") The American editor of Meyer's *Commentary* adds his own comment to the one quoted above from Calvin, saying in part: "By the Holy Ghost here we do not understand the regenerating and·sanctifying agency of the Holy Spirit in the conversion and renewal of the soul; the impartation of such a presence of the Holy Spirit as is accompanied with super-natural gifts; the miraculous influences of the Spirit, which were manifested by speaking with tongues, or other visible tokens" (p. 180). Note the evidence here for two distinct acts of the Holy Spirit in regeneration and filling.

2. Acts 9 is another record of the same spiritual phenomenon. Briefly let me summarize a portion of it. Saul met Jesus in the "theophany" on the Damascus road, and the context indicates that he was saved (regenerated) in this encounter with the living Son of God. After spending three days in fasting and prayer, Ananias was sent to Saul, and his greeting in Acts 9:17 tells us a great deal about Saul's spiritual condition. "And Ananias departed, and entered into the house; and laying his hands on him said, Brother Saul, the Lord, even Jesus, who appeared unto thee in the way which thou camest, hath sent me, that thou mayest receive thy sight, and be filled with the Holy Spirit." From the preceding context, it is clear that Ananias knew who Saul was, and also that he had come to Damascus to persecute the Christians there. Ananias would, therefore, never have entered Saul's presence, and addressed him as "Brother Saul," unless he knew that Saul was, in very truth, "a brother in Christ." Saul must, therefore, have become a Christian, in the fullest sense of the word, before Ananias went in to him. Now notice that Saul received the healing of his sight and the infilling of the Holy Spirit when Ananias laid his hands upon him. Clearly then, Saul's conversion, and subsequent infilling (baptism) in the Holy Spirit, show again the two distinct and separate acts of the Holy Spirit in conversion (regeneration) and filling (or baptism).

Allow me to digress here for a little. It is frequently urged at this point that Paul did not speak in "tongues" when Ananias laid hands on him, and he was filled with the Holy Spirit. Since Acts 9:17-19 is silent on this point, there is, I suppose, room for polemic jockeying. But please consider Paul's own testimony on this subject. He says, I Cor. 14:14: "I thank God, I speak with tongues more than you all . . ." Whether Paul spoke in tongues immediately when he was filled (baptized) with the Holy Spirit, by the laying on of Ananias' hands, or subsequently, is of small consequence here. He did speak in tongues (and I pray that those who are so virulently opposed to speaking in tongues would ponder Paul's attitude toward this supernatural manifestation of the Holy Spirit, viz., "I thank my God, I speak with tongues more than ye all").

Furthermore, the book of Acts makes it quite clear that speaking in tongues (i.e., other languages given supernaturally by the Holy Spirit) is a consequence of the baptism in the Holy Spirit.

Let us return to the main thread of our discussion. The following is a third example from the book of Acts of the Scriptural foundation of my position in this matter.

3. In Acts 19:1-7, Paul met certain disciples of John the Baptist, at Ephesus. He expounded the gospel more accurately to them, and then baptized them in the name of Jesus. Acts 19:4, 5

records it thus: "And Paul said, John baptized with the baptism of repentance, saying unto the people that they should believe on him that should come after him, that is on Jesus. And when they heard this, they were baptized into the name of the Lord Jesus." Here again we find "believers' baptism" clearly spelled out for us. We can be sure that Paul would not have baptized them in water unless he had reasonable assurance of their conversion (regeneration). Observe carefully the sequel, as written in Acts 19:6: "And when Paul had laid his hands upon them, the Holy Spirit came on them; and they spake with tongues, and prophesied." Again we see two distinct operations of the Holy Spirit in conversion (regeneration) and filling (baptizing).

There are other examples found in the book of Acts, but these are sufficient to demonstrate that my position is broadly based in the relevant Scriptures.

Sincerely yours in Christ,
s/ Pastor Ervin

RECORDS

order from your local bookstore
or W.B.S.
Box 292
Watchung, N.J. 07061

GOD IS FOR THE EMOTIONALLY ILL —Guldseth	A507	.95
YOUTH WITH A MISSION— Wilson	A152	1.25
ONCE A JUNKIE—Arguinzoni	A509	1.25
GOD'S LIVING ROOM—Walker	A123	.95
GONE IS SHADOWS' CHILD—Foy	L337	.95
GRACE AND THE GLORY OF GOD —Benson/Jarman	L104	1.50
HEALING ADVENTURE—White	L345	1.95
HEALING LIGHT—Sanford	L726	1.25
HEAR MY CONFESSION—Orsini	L341	1.00
HEY GOD!—Foglio	P007	1.95
HOLY SPIRIT AND YOU—Bennett	L324	2.50
JESUS AND ISRAEL—Benson	A514	.95
JESUS PEOPLE ARE COMING—King	L340	1.95
JESUS PEOPLE—Pederson	AA2	.95
LAYMAN'S GUIDE TO HOLY SPIRIT—Rea	L387	2.50
LET THIS CHURCH DIE—Weaver	A520	.95
LIFE IN THE HOLY SPIRIT—Harper	5F	.50
LONELY NOW—Cruz	A510	1.25
LORD OF THE VALLEYS—Bulle	L018	2.50
LOST SHEPHERD—Sanford	L328	.95
MADE ALIVE— Price	P001	1.50
MANIFEST VICTORY—Moseley	L724	2.50
MIRACLES THROUGH PRAYER—Harrell	A518	.95
NICKY CRUZ GIVES THE FACTS ON DRUGS —Cruz	B70	.50
NINE O'CLOCK IN THE MORNING—Bennett	P555	2.50
NONE CAN GUESS—Harper	L722	1.95
OUT OF THIS WORLD—Fisher	A517	.95
OVERFLOWING LIFE—Frost	L327	1.75
PATHWAY TO POWER—Davison	L00X	1.50
PENTECOSTALS—Nichol	LH711	2.50

SUGGESTED INEXPENSIVE PAPERBACK BOOKS
WHEREVER PAPERBACKS ARE SOLD

A NEW SONG—Boone	AA3	$ .95
AGLOW WITH THE SPIRIT—Frost	L326	1.25
AMAZING SAINTS—Saint	L409	2.50
AND FORBID NOT TO SPEAK—Ervin	L329	.95
AND SIGNS FOLLOWED—Price	P002	1.50
ANGELS OF LIGHT?—Freeman	A506	1.25
ANSWERS TO PRAISE—Carothers	L670	1.95
ARMSTRONG ERROR—DeLoach	L317	.95
AS AT THE BEGINNING—Harper	L721	.95
BAPTISM IN THE SPIRIT—Schep	L343	1.50
BAPTISM IN THE SPIRIT—BIBLICAL —Cockburn	16F	.65
BAPTISM OF FIRE—Harper	8F	.60
BAPTIZED IN ONE SPIRIT—Baker	1F	.60
BEN ISRAEL—Katz	A309	.95
BLACK TRACKS—Miles	A298	.95
BORN TO BURN—Wallace	A508	.95
CHALLENGING COUNTERFEIT—Gasson	L102	.95
COMING ALIVE—Buckingham	A501	.95
CONFESSIONS OF A HERETIC—Hunt	L31X	2.50
COUNSELOR TO COUNSELOR—Campbell	L335	1.50
CRISIS AMERICA—Otis	AA1	.95
DAYSPRING—White	L334	1.95
DISCOVERY (Booklet)—Frost	F71	.50
ERA OF THE SPIRIT—Williams	L322	1.95
15 STEPS OUT—Mumford	L106	1.50
FROM THE BELLY OF THE WHALE—White	A318	.95
GATHERED FOR POWER—Pulkingham	AA4	2.50
GOD BREAKS IN—Congdon	L313	1.95

PIONEERS OF REVIVAL—Clarke	L723	.95
POWER IN PRAISE—Carothers	L342	1.95
POWER FOR THE BODY—Harper	4F	.85
PREACHER WITH A BILLY CLUB—Asmuth	A209	.95
PRISON TO PRAISE—Carothers	A504	1.25
PROPHECY A GIFT FOR THE BODY—Harper	2F	.65
PSEUDO CHRISTIANS—Jarman	A516	.95
REAL FAITH—Price	P000	1.50
RUN BABY RUN—Cruz	L101	1.25
RUN BABY RUN—Cruz (Comic Book)		.20
SATAN SELLERS—Warnke	L794	2.50
SOUL PATROL—Bartlett	A500	.95
SPEAKING WITH GOD—Cantelon	L336	.95
SPIRIT BADE ME GO—DuPlessis	L325	.95
SPIRITUAL AND PHYSICAL HEALING —Price	P003	1.95
SPIRITUAL WARFARE—Harper	A505	.95
STRONGER THAN PRISON WALLS —Wurmbrand	A956	.95
TAKE ANOTHER LOOK—Mumford	L338	2.50
THERE'S MORE—Hall	L344	1.50
THESE ARE NOT DRUNKEN—Ervin	L105	2.50
THIS EARTH'S END—Benson	A513	.95
THIS WHICH YE SEE AND HEAR—Ervin	L728	1.95
TONGUES UNDER FIRE—Lillie	3F	.85
TURN YOUR BACK ON THE PROBLEM —Smith	L034	1.95
TWO WORLDS—Price	P004	1.95
UNDERGROUND SAINTS—Wurmbrand	U-1	.95
WALK IN THE SPIRIT—Harper	L319	.95
WE'VE BEEN ROBBED—Meloon	L339	1.50
YOU CAN KNOW GOD—Price	P005	.75
YOUR NEW LOOK—Buckingham	A503	.95

FREE SAMPLE COPY OF

LOGOS

An International Charismatic Journal

Worldwide Coverage
Feature Articles
Book Reviews
Trends

Write to:

LOGOS
185 NORTH AVENUE
PLAINFIELD, NEW JERSEY 07060

SEND:

☐ **FREE Sample**

☐ or **ONE-YEAR Subscription** ($4.00)

Name_____
Address_____
City_____State_____Zip_____